NFL's TOP 10 PLAYS

by Dan Myers

NFL's
TOP TEN

SportsZone

An Imprint of Abdo Publishing
abdopublishing.com

abdopublishing.com

Published by Abdo Publishing, a division of ABDO, PO Box 398166, Minneapolis, Minnesota 55439. Copyright © 2018 by Abdo Consulting Group, Inc. International copyrights reserved in all countries. No part of this book may be reproduced in any form without written permission from the publisher. SportsZone™ is a trademark and logo of Abdo Publishing.

Printed in the United States of America, North Mankato, Minnesota
042017
092017

THIS BOOK CONTAINS
RECYCLED MATERIALS

Cover Photo: Gene Puskar/AP Images
Interior Photos: Andrew Harnik/AP Images, 4–5; Patrick Semansky/AP Images, 6–7; David Goldman/AP Images, 8–9; David J. Phillip/AP Images, 9, 25; John Bazemore/AP Images, 10; Charlie Riedel/AP Images, 11, 27; Ted S. Warren/AP Images, 12–13; Elise Amendola/AP Images, 14–15; AP Images, 17; Dick Raphael/Sports Illustrated/Getty Images, 18; Harry Cabluck/AP Images, 19; Al Messerschmidt/AP Images, 21; Peter Read Miller/AP Images, 22–23; AJ Mast/AP Images, 24–25; Julie Jacobson/AP Images, 26

Editor: Patrick Donnelly
Series Designer: Craig Hinton

Publisher's Cataloging-in-Publication Data

Names: Myers, Dan, author.
Title: NFL's top ten plays / by Dan Myers.
Description: Minneapolis, MN : Abdo Publishing, 2018. | Series: NFL's top 10 |
    Includes bibliographical references and index.
Identifiers: LCCN 2016963094 | ISBN 9781532111419 (lib. bdg.) |
    ISBN 9781680789263 (ebook)
Subjects: LCSH: National Football League--Juvenile literature. | Football--
    --United States--History--Juvenile literature. | Football--United States--
    Miscellanea--Juvenile literature. | Football--United States--Statistics--Juvenile
    literature.
Classification: DDC 796.332--dc23
LC record available at http://lccn.loc.gov/201693094

Table of
CONTENTS

Introduction

National Football League (NFL) games often are decided by one play. Sometimes it's the last play of the game—a long touchdown pass or a game-saving tackle. Sometimes a player changes the outcome with a big play earlier in the game.

Fans love to talk about those plays. They share videos of them online. They talk about them with their friends. And they'll remember them for years to come. Many of the plays picked up nicknames of their own, from "The Catch" to "The Immaculate Reception," further cementing their place in the memories of sports fans.

Read on to learn more about some of the greatest plays in NFL history.

10

Julian Edelman, *11*, gets his hands under the ball just before it hits the turf as Keanu Neal, *22*, and Ricardo Allen fight for possession.

Tip Drill

Catching a deflected pass requires a bit of luck, to be sure. But it also requires quick thinking, lightning-fast reflexes, and sure hands.

And if it's in the final minutes of the Super Bowl and the offense is trying to march the length of the field for a chance to send the game into overtime? Then it requires tremendous grace under pressure.

Julian Edelman displayed all of those elements as he made a remarkable catch in Super Bowl LI in February 2017.

Edelman's New England Patriots trailed the Atlanta Falcons 28–20. The Patriots got the ball at their own 9-yard line with 3:30 to play. They needed to score a touchdown and make a two-point conversion to force overtime.

Quarterback Tom Brady completed two passes to get the ball out to the New England 36. Then he fired a pass over the middle to Edelman. But Brady's throw was a bit too low. Falcons cornerback Robert Alford leaped for the ball, and it glanced off his fingertips.

As the ball tumbled to the turf, Atlanta safeties Keanu Neal and Ricardo Allen closed in on it. But Edelman didn't give up. He made a dive for the ball, too, and was able to grab it as it bounced off Alford's leg. The ball came loose again, but Edelman secured it just before it hit the ground.

Edelman shouted "I caught it!" The officials reviewed the play. They agreed—it was a catch. New England had the ball at Atlanta's 41-yard line.

COMEBACK KINGS

Edelman's catch was just part of a record-setting comeback. The Patriots trailed 28–3 in the third quarter but scored 25 straight points to force overtime. Then they marched down the field on the first possession of overtime and scored the game-winning touchdown. No team had ever overcome a deficit of more than 10 points in Super Bowl history.

Four plays later, the Patriots were in the end zone. Edelman's amazing play made it all possible.

09

The Butler Did It

Quarterback Tom Brady usually gets a lot of credit when the New England Patriots win games. But when the Patriots won the Super Bowl after the 2014 season, an undrafted rookie cornerback made the biggest play.

The Patriots were clinging to a 28–24 lead over the Seattle Seahawks. Seattle had the ball on third down at New England's 1-yard line with 26 seconds to play. And the Seahawks had running back Marshawn Lynch, one of the best power runners in the NFL.

The call seemed simple: hand the ball to Lynch and let him bull his way into the end zone for the game-winning touchdown.

But Seahawks head coach Pete Carroll had other ideas. He thought the Patriots defenders would expect a run. So he decided to surprise them.

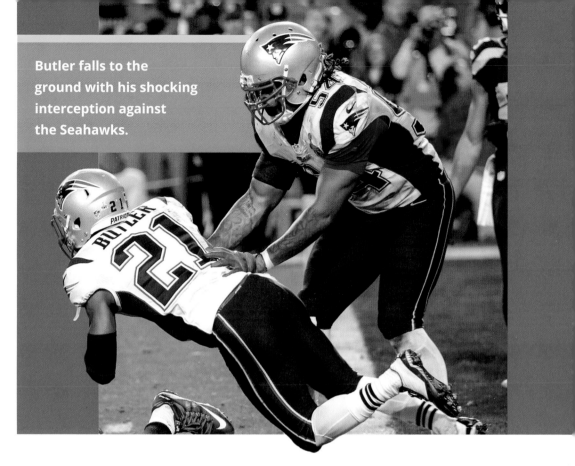

Quarterback Russell Wilson brought the Seahawks to the line of scrimmage. He had two receivers to his right. On the other side of the ball, rookie cornerback Malcolm Butler recognized the formation. He thought the Seahawks might throw the ball.

Wilson took the snap and fired a quick pass toward receiver Ricardo Lockette. Butler jumped in front of Lockette and snatched the ball out of the air. Lockette slammed into him, but Butler held on for the most famous interception in Super Bowl history.

Butler hadn't even been drafted after completing his college career at tiny West Alabama. He made the Patriots' roster as a rookie free agent. He ended his first pro season as a Super Bowl hero. Brady won the Super Bowl MVP Award. But without Butler's big play, the Patriots likely wouldn't have won their fourth Super Bowl in team history.

08

James Harrison is exhausted by his 100-yard jaunt.

Going the Distance

Pittsburgh Steelers linebacker James Harrison was known more for hitting people than outrunning them. But he left behind all 11 Arizona Cardinals during one memorable interception return.

The Steelers and Cardinals were playing in the Super Bowl in February 2009. With 18 seconds left in the first half, the Steelers led 10–7. But the Cardinals had the ball at the Pittsburgh 2-yard line. Poised to grab the lead before halftime, the Cardinals saw momentum swing on just one play.

Cardinals quarterback Kurt Warner threw a pass to receiver Anquan Boldin at the goal line. But Harrison read Warner's eyes perfectly and stepped in front of the pass for an interception.

That's where the linebacker's long rumble began.

Harrison, not known for his speed, took off. He angled toward the sideline and broke two tackles, including one try by Warner.

Larry Fitzgerald, *left*, tries to tackle Harrison before he reaches the end zone.

HOLMES HAULS IN WINNER

The Cardinals came back to take the lead, but the Steelers won their sixth Super Bowl on another amazing play. Trailing by three points with 42 seconds remaining, Pittsburgh quarterback Ben Roethlisberger took the snap at the Arizona 6-yard line. He scrambled to his right to buy time before throwing to the back corner of the end zone. Receiver Santonio Holmes caught the pass and got both feet down barely in bounds for the touchdown. Pittsburgh won 27–23.

Teammates caught up and began blocking for him. Harrison cruised past midfield. Cardinals running back Tim Hightower raced down the field and had a good angle to make a tackle. But Harrison cut inside as one of his teammates sent Hightower sprawling.

Now 70 yards from where he caught the ball, Harrison lost some speed. Near the 10-yard line he dodged another tackle attempt by Arizona lineman Mike Gandy. Wide receivers Larry Fitzgerald and Steve Breaston finally slammed into Harrison inside the 5-yard line. Fitzgerald tried to strip the ball away. But Harrison would not be denied. He crashed across the goal line for a touchdown as the clock reached zero.

07

The Richter Scale Run

Scientists use the Richter Scale to explain how strong earthquakes are. Thanks to Marshawn Lynch, NFL fans found another use for it.

The Seattle Seahawks were hosting the New Orleans Saints in a playoff game after the 2010 season. With 3:37 to play, the Seahawks had the ball at their own 33-yard line, leading by four points. Their raucous fans were on their feet hoping the hometown team could put together a scoring drive and close out a big victory.

What they saw next was one of the greatest runs in NFL history.

Seahawks quarterback Matt Hasselbeck took the snap and handed off to Lynch. The running back was supposed to go right up the middle—a simple play called "17 Power." The idea was mainly to run time off the clock.

It did a lot more than that. Lynch took the handoff and blasted through the line of scrimmage. He ran over two Saints defenders, then broke through two arm tackles. He slipped another tackle and cut to his right toward the sideline. Cornerback Tracy Porter

Marshawn Lynch, *left*, prepares to drop Tracy Porter with a stiff-arm on the way to his 67-yard touchdown rumble.

tried to bring Lynch down at the Saints 35-yard line. But Lynch used his free hand to fling the smaller Porter to the ground.

Once he reached the sideline, Lynch broke toward the end zone. He eluded one more diving tackler at the 15-yard line. Finally, he outran three defenders to the goal line and leaped into the end zone for the score.

In all, Lynch broke eight tackles on his way to the end zone. Seattle fans erupted. Their jumping and cheering created enough energy to register a tremor at a local station that tracks earthquakes.

06

John Elway, 7, spins between three Green Bay defenders as he dives for a first down. →

The Helicopter Run

Denver Broncos quarterback John Elway was in the twilight of his career in 1997. He had already been on the losing end of three Super Bowls. But at age 37, Elway had an outstanding season. He threw a career-high 27 touchdown passes and led the Broncos back to the Super Bowl.

Denver faced the defending champion Green Bay Packers. Green Bay was heavily favored, but no one could account for Elway's desire to finally win a Super Bowl. One play demonstrated just how far that desire could carry Elway and the Broncos.

The game was tied 17–17 late in the third quarter. Denver had the ball at the Green Bay 12-yard line. It was third down with six yards to go for a first down.

Elway dropped back to pass, but his receivers were covered. He had no choice but to tuck the ball away and run. Three Packers converged on him near the 5-yard line. But instead of safely sliding to the ground and avoiding a hit, Elway dove forward to get as many yards as he could. The defenders slammed into Elway, spinning his body like the rotors of a helicopter.

Elway landed with a thud at the 4-yard line. His 8-yard gain gave Denver a first down and kept the drive alive. Two plays later,

running back Terrell Davis scored a touchdown to give the Broncos a
24–17 lead.

While Elway's play didn't win the game, it showed what the 15-year
veteran was willing to do in order to win a championship. Denver
ended up winning 31–24, giving Elway and the Broncos their first Super
Bowl victory.

05

The Starr Sneak

It was a cold New Year's Eve day in northeast Wisconsin. The Dallas Cowboys were battling the Green Bay Packers in the 1967 NFL Championship Game at Lambeau Field. Temperatures were well below zero Fahrenheit (minus-18°C) throughout the game, which became known as the "Ice Bowl."

With 16 seconds left in the game, the Cowboys led 17–14. The Packers had the ball on the Dallas 1-yard line. It was third down, but Green Bay was out of timeouts.

For legendary Packers coach Vince Lombardi, there was one clear option. He put the game in the capable hands of Hall of Fame quarterback Bart Starr.

Starr called a handoff to the fullback. But Starr told nobody that he had a different plan in mind. On an icy field, with five-time All-Pro guard Jerry Kramer in front of him, Starr believed it would be easiest to keep the ball himself.

Kramer and center Ken Bowman double-teamed Cowboys defensive tackle Jethro Pugh. They pushed him back enough to make a hole for Starr, who lunged across the goal line for a touchdown. The Packers won 21–17 and went on to win the Super Bowl for their third straight NFL championship.

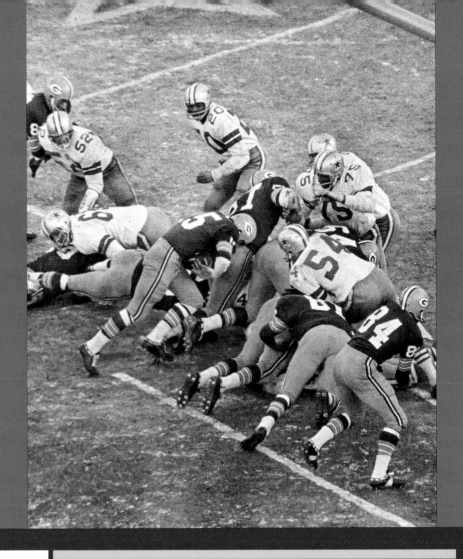

SAN FRANCISCO SCRAMBLE

Steve Young was one of the fastest and most elusive quarterbacks of all time. The San Francisco 49ers star put his running skills on display against the Minnesota Vikings in 1988. With the ball at the Vikings 49-yard line, Young dropped back to pass. Finding no open receivers, he spun away from three Vikings and took off running. Young cut to his left, avoiding two more defenders, then outran a third. Over the final 40 yards, getting blocks from his teammates, he ran through three other tackles before stumbling into the end zone.

04

Franco Harris slips past Oakland's last defender, Jimmy Warren, on the way to the end zone.

The Immaculate Reception

On December 23, 1972, the Pittsburgh Steelers got an early Christmas present.

The Steelers were trailing the Oakland Raiders 7–6 with time running out in a playoff game at Pittsburgh's Three Rivers Stadium. It was fourth down and 10 yards to go with just 22 seconds to play. Pittsburgh was on its own 40-yard line.

Needing a miracle, Steelers quarterback Terry Bradshaw dropped back to pass. The Raiders pressured him immediately. Bradshaw eluded two players, then heaved a pass downfield toward teammate Frenchy Fuqua.

Raiders safety Jack Tatum was in position. He crushed Fuqua as the ball arrived. The collision sent the ball sailing back toward the line of scrimmage.

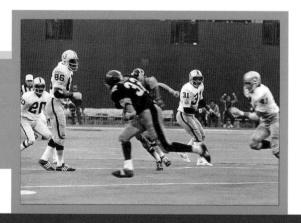

Harris, *32*, heads toward the sideline after picking up the pass deflected by Jack Tatum, *31*.

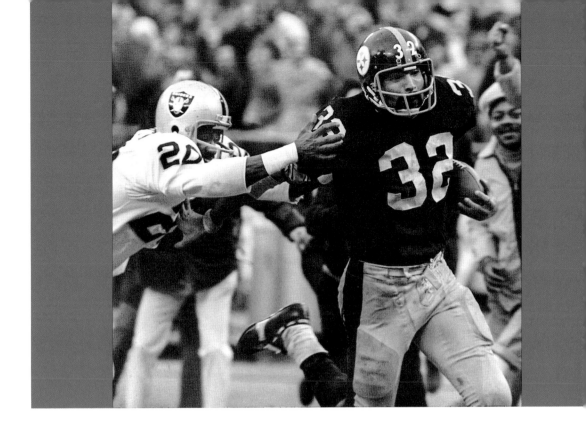

But the Steelers weren't through. Seemingly out of nowhere, Pittsburgh running back Franco Harris arrived on the scene. He caught the ball just before it hit the ground. The Raiders were stunned. Harris took off down the sideline, outrunning three Raiders to reach the end zone.

This was in the days before officials used instant replay to review plays. Referee Fred Swearingen huddled his crew together to discuss what had just happened. Had the ball touched the ground? Had Tatum touched the ball? If it had deflected off Fuqua, the rule at the time said Harris couldn't be the next person to touch it. After a short delay, Swearingen raised his hands in the air for a touchdown.

The Raiders were outraged. But their arguments didn't change the call. The Steelers won the game 13–7 thanks to the play known as the "Immaculate Reception."

03

Kevin Dyson, *87*, is escorted to the end zone by his teammates after catching Frank Wycheck's lateral.

The Music City Miracle

Buffalo Bills kicker Steve Christie teed up the football for a simple kickoff. He had no way of predicting the mayhem that was about to follow.

Christie had just kicked a field goal to give the Bills a 16–15 lead over the Tennessee Titans. Just 20 seconds remained in their playoff game at Tennessee on January 8, 2000. A kickoff and a play or two on defense were all that stood between the Bills and a big upset over the heavily favored Titans.

Christie kicked the ball high in the air but not very far. Tennessee fullback Lorenzo Neal caught it on the Titans 25-yard line. He ran to his right, then handed the ball to tight end Frank Wycheck. Wycheck took a few more steps to the right. Then he turned and threw a pass back to his left that sailed into the arms of teammate Kevin Dyson near the opposite sideline.

The Bills had converged on Wycheck. They weren't expecting him to throw. Dyson had blockers in front of him and room to run. He sprinted down the sideline. Only Christie stood between Dyson and the end zone. But the Titans had three blockers, easily paving a path for a touchdown.

RAM TOUGH

On January 30, 2000, the Titans stood 10 yards from forcing overtime in the Super Bowl. Quarterback Steve McNair took the snap and hit Dyson streaking toward the end zone. All that stood between him and the goal line was St. Louis Rams linebacker Mike Jones. Dyson bolted toward the end zone, but Jones got a hold of his legs, bringing him down at the 1-yard line as time expired. The Rams won 23–16.

Referees reviewed whether Wycheck's pass had gone forward. A forward pass would have been illegal and the touchdown would not have counted. After looking at the replay, officials confirmed that it was a backwards pass, and the touchdown stood. The "Music City Miracle" gave the Titans an amazing 22–16 victory. They went on to play in their first Super Bowl that year.

02

Dwight Clark spikes the ball after scoring the touchdown that lifted the 49ers past Dallas.

The Catch

The Dallas Cowboys were NFL royalty throughout the 1970s. They played in five Super Bowls in the decade and won two of them. Meanwhile, the San Francisco 49ers were one of the league's worst teams. They endured back-to-back 2–14 seasons in 1978 and 1979.

That changed just two years later. The 49ers kicked off a new dynasty in the Bay Area, and they did so by knocking off the Cowboys.

On January 10, 1982, the 49ers hosted the Cowboys with a Super Bowl berth on the line. With just under five minutes left, San Francisco trailed by six points and needed to drive 89 yards for the go-ahead touchdown.

Quarterback Joe Montana drove the 49ers down the field. They reached the Dallas 6-yard line. It was third down. Montana rolled to his right. He kept shuffling his feet until he was almost to the sideline, trying to give his receivers time to get open while he avoided the Cowboys pass rush. Finally, Montana launched a pass toward the back of the end zone.

The ball appeared to be headed well beyond the back of the end zone. But wide receiver Dwight Clark was there. He leapt

high, stretching his 6-foot-4-inch frame as far as he could, and made the catch—or "The Catch," as it came to be known around the NFL. The play tied the game at 27 with 51 seconds to play.

San Francisco kicker Ray Wersching kicked the extra point to give the 49ers a one-point lead with 47 seconds to play. Dallas got the ball back and advanced to midfield, but quarterback Danny White was sacked, and he fumbled. The Niners recovered, sealing the victory. They went on to win the Super Bowl, the first of four titles in the 1980s for the former NFL doormat.

01

Tom Brady and the Patriots' record-setting offense were riding high going into the Super Bowl.

The Helmet Catch

The greatest plays in NFL history often are made on the biggest stage in the world.

In 2007 the New England Patriots dominated the NFL. They outscored their opponents by almost 20 points per game as they rolled to the first undefeated regular season by any NFL team in 35 years. After two playoff victories, all they needed was a Super Bowl victory to match the 1972 Miami Dolphins as the only unbeaten Super Bowl champions.

The New York Giants were an unlikely opponent. The Giants had gone 10–6 in the regular season and barely reached the playoffs as a wild card. But three road playoff victories earned them a trip to the Super Bowl to face the Patriots.

The Giants were heavy underdogs, but they kept it close throughout the game. New England scored to take a 14–10 lead

Lawrence Tynes kicked the Giants into the Super Bowl with an overtime field goal at Green Bay.

with 2:42 to play. All the Patriots needed was one more defensive stand to make history.

But New York quarterback Eli Manning led his team back down the field. Starting at their own 17-yard line, the Giants moved to their own 44. It was third down and five yards to go. Manning took the snap and was immediately under pressure. The Patriots defensive line pushed hard, quickly collapsing the pocket. Manning stepped forward as a Patriots pass rusher grabbed him.

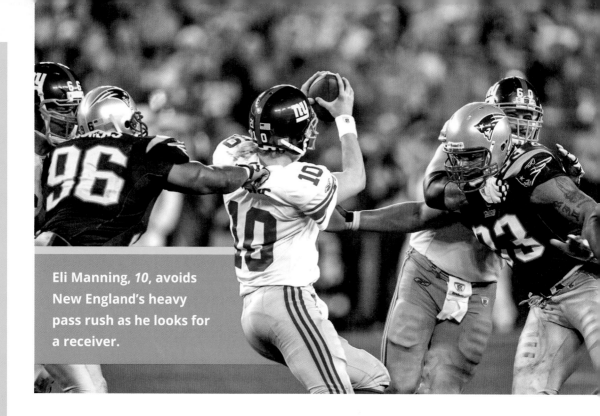

Eli Manning, *10*, avoids New England's heavy pass rush as he looks for a receiver.

But Manning refused to go down. He managed to wriggle free and escape to his right. With two Patriots zeroing in on him, Manning launched a pass down the middle of the field.

Standing at the New England 25-yard line, Giants wide receiver David Tyree fought for position. He saw that the ball was headed high. With a man covering him, Tyree jumped as high as he could. Both of his arms were extended above his head.

The ball hit Tyree's hands. But Patriots safety Rodney Harrison, who was covering Tyree, grabbed the receiver's right arm, separating it from the ball for an instant.

With only one hand free, Tyree pinned the ball to his helmet long enough to rip his other hand away from Harrison. As Tyree landed on the ground, he held the ball against his helmet. The ball was just inches above the turf, but it never touched the ground. The referee signaled it was a

BLIZZARD BLASTS

Kickers aren't supposed to like snow, but it didn't seem to bother Adam Vinatieri in the 2001 playoffs. Playing in a wicked New England blizzard, the Patriots kicker blasted a low line drive through the wind and snow and just over the crossbar. The 45-yard field goal sent the game against the Oakland Raiders to overtime tied 13–13. Then Vinatieri drilled a 23-yard kick to win it for New England. The Patriots went on to win their first Super Bowl, starting a new NFL dynasty.

David Tyree holds on despite the best efforts of safety Rodney Harrison.

catch. The 32-yard completion gave the Giants a first down at the Patriots 24-yard line. New York had new life.

Four plays later, Manning hit wide receiver Plaxico Burress in the end zone for a 13-yard touchdown. The Giants held on to win 17–14, pulling off one of the biggest upsets in Super Bowl history.

Honorable Mentions

HOLY ROLLER: On September 10, 1978, the Oakland Raiders defeated the San Diego Chargers in one of the most controversial endings in NFL history. The Raiders trailed by six points with 10 seconds left. Quarterback Ken Stabler dropped back to pass and was under immediate pressure. As he was being sacked, Stabler fumbled the ball toward the goal line. There was a scramble for the ball near the 10-yard line, but it got kicked into the end zone. Finally, Raiders tight end Dave Casper jumped on the ball. The play was ruled a touchdown. Did Stabler intentionally fumble? Was it an underhand pass? At the time, teams could advance a forward fumble, as long as it was unintentional. Not long after the play, the NFL changed the rules. Players could no longer advance any fumble in the final two minutes of a half. Had that rule existed before, the Chargers would have won. Instead, Oakland kicked the extra point and won 21–20.

BAYOU BLOCK: Hurricane Katrina devastated the city of New Orleans in 2005. The New Orleans Saints' stadium, the Superdome, was in ruins, and thousands of their fans were homeless and displaced. The Saints played home games in three different cities that season. When they returned to New Orleans for the first time in 2006, the Saints gave their fans something to cheer about. Less than two minutes into their first game back, New Orleans safety Steve Gleason blocked an Atlanta Falcons punt. The Saints recovered for a touchdown and went on to win the game. The play became a symbol of the city's spirit and determination to come back. Gleason's punt block has been immortalized as a statue in front of the Superdome.

LOOK MA, ONE HAND: In 2014 New York Giants rookie wide receiver Odell Beckham Jr. made a catch for the ages. Quarterback Eli Manning launched a long pass down the sideline. Beckham jostled for position with Dallas Cowboys cornerback Brandon Carr. Near the goal line, Beckham jumped and stretched his right arm as far as he could. He snatched the ball out of the air with just his fingertips and fell back into the end zone. Amazingly he held onto the ball with one hand throughout the play, scoring a touchdown on one of the most amazing catches of all time.

HAIL AARON: In a 2015 game at Detroit, the Green Bay Packers trailed the Lions 23–21 with time for one last play. Packers quarterback Aaron Rodgers took the snap at his own 39-yard line. He danced around long enough for his receivers to get to the end zone. Then Rodgers heaved the ball 65 yards in the air. Packers tight end Richard Rodgers came down with it in the end zone, giving Green Bay a shocking victory.

MOSS HYSTERIA: Randy Moss made some circus catches in his day. But he's also remembered for a pass he made. In a 2003 game at the Metrodome, the Minnesota Vikings and Denver Broncos appeared to be headed to halftime tied 7–7. But on the last play of the half, Vikings quarterback Daunte Culpepper launched a pass from his own 40-yard line. Moss caught it at the Denver 10 and was immediately surrounded by four Broncos defenders. As he was being tackled, Moss flipped the ball over his shoulder to teammate Moe Williams, who scampered into the end zone for a touchdown. The Vikings went on to win 28–20.

Glossary

cornerback
A defensive player who normally covers wide receivers.

elude
To avoid or get away from.

favored
Expected to win.

line of scrimmage
The place on the field where a play starts.

momentum
A force, either positive or negative, that seems to pull a team in one direction.

pocket
The area behind the line of scrimmage where the quarterback stands after dropping back to pass.

raucous
Rowdy, hard to control.

reflexes
Actions that are performed as a response to a stimulus and without conscious thought.

rotors
The part of an aircraft that rotates to generate lift and thrust.

underdog
The person or team that is not expected to win.

wild card
A team that makes the playoffs even though it did not win its division.

For More Information

Books

Mason, Tyler. *Football Trivia*. Minneapolis, MN: Abdo Publishing, 2016.

Rivkin, Jennifer. *Gridiron Greats: Heroes of Football*. New York: Crabtree, 2016.

Scheff, Matt. *The Best NFL Quarterbacks of All Time*. Minneapolis, MN: Abdo Publishing, 2014.

Websites

To learn more about the NFL, visit **abdobooklinks.com**. These links are routinely monitored and updated to provide the most current information available.

Place to Visit

Pro Football Hall of Fame

2121 George Halas Drive NW
Canton, Ohio 44708
330-456-8207
www.profootballhof.com

The Hall of Fame is like a museum dedicated to football. There are exhibits on the origins of the game, artifacts from famous moments, and busts honoring the greatest players and coaches ever.

Index

About the Author

Dan Myers was raised in Eagan, Minnesota, and graduated with a degree in journalism from Minnesota State University. He has covered sports at all levels in the Twin Cities since 2008. He and his wife live in Hudson, Wisconsin, with their beagle, Kato.